ESSENTIAL ELEMENTS 2000

COMPREHENSIVE BAND METHOD

TIM LAUTZENHEISER   **JOHN HIGGINS**   **CHARLES MENGHINI**
PAUL LAVENDER   **TOM C. RHODES**   **DON BIERSCHENK**

CONGRATULATIONS and welcome to ***Essential Elements 2000 – Book 2!***

PLAY ALONG CD DISC 1

Your book includes the **Play Along CD Disc 1** which covers two different sections of Book 2:

- The first 55 exercises   —*and*—

- The Individual Study section (pages 38–41)

During the first 55 exercises, the melody is demonstrated by a small band ensemble. A professional soloist is featured **playing your instrument** for the Individual Study section.

Each track begins with a one measure count-off, and it is played **twice**—the second time is the accompaniment-only. These track accompaniments are performed by professional studio musicians, and they explore a rich variety of musical styles and cultures, with classical, rock, jazz, country, and world music.

PLAY ALONG CD SET – DISC 2 & 3

This set of play-along tracks is available from your music dealer, and includes exercise 56 through the end of Book 2. It features the melody demonstrated by a small band ensemble, followed by the accompaniment-only. For use by all instruments.

ISBN 0-634-01300-9

Copyright © 2004 by HAL LEONARD CORPORATION

International Copyright Secured   All Rights Reserved

HAL•LEONARD® CORPORATION

7777 W. BLUEMOUND RD. P.O. BOX 13819 MILWAUKEE, WI 53213

REVIEW

KEY SIGNATURE   **TIME SIGNATURES**

Key of B♭

NOTES	Whole	Half	Quarter	Eighths
RESTS				

REPEAT SIGN   **TIE**   **TEMPO MARKINGS**

Allegro
Moderato

1. TECHNIQUE TRAX

2. SHOO FLY

American Folk Song

Allegro

3. THAILAND LULLABY

Thai Folk Song

Moderato

4. SHEPHERD'S HEY

English Folk Song

Moderato

5. THE CRAWDAD SONG

American Folk Song

Allegro

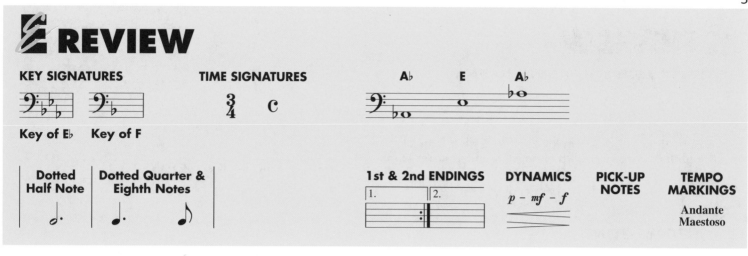

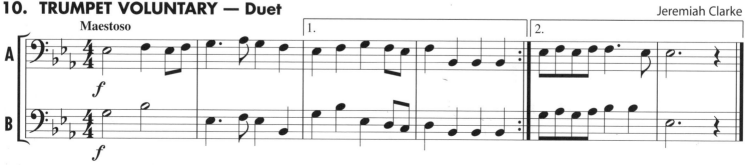

REVIEW

Staccato

Staccato notes are played lightly and with separation. They are marked with a dot above or below the note.

15. TREADING LIGHTLY

Moderato

Tenuto

Tenuto notes are played smoothly and connected, holding each note until the next is played. They are marked with a straight line above or below the note.

Slur

A curved line which connects notes of different pitch.

Hammer on — Is achieved by plucking the first note of a slurred passage with the right hand, then pressing down the second note with the left hand.

Pull off — Is achieved by plucking the first note of a slurred passage with the right hand, then releasing the first note with the left hand enabling the second note to ring.

16. SMOOTH MOVE

Moderato

5th fret D string

17. SHIFTING GEARS

Moderato

English composer **Thomas Tallis** (1508–1585) served as a royal court composer for Kings Henry VIII and Edward VI, and Queens Mary and Elizabeth. During Tallis' lifetime, the artist Michaelangelo painted the Sistine Chapel.

Canons (one or more parts imitating the first part) were used in many forms by 16th century composers. A **Round** is a strict (or exact) canon which can be repeated any number of times without stopping. Play *Tallis Canon* as a 4-part round.

HISTORY

18. TALLIS CANON (Round)

Moderato

Thomas Tallis

Sightreading

Sightreading means playing a musical piece for the first time. The key to sightreading success is to know what to look for *before* you play. Use the word **S-T-A-R-S** to remind yourself what to look for, and eventually your band will become sightreading STARS!

S — **Sharps or flats** in the key signature
T — **Time signature** and **tempo markings**
A — **Accidentals** not found in the key signature
R — **Rhythms**, silently counting the more difficult notes and rests
S — **Signs**, including dynamics, articulations, repeats and endings

19. SIGHTREADING CHALLENGE

Moderato

5th fret A string

5th fret D string

DAILY WARM-UPS

WORK-OUTS FOR TONE & TECHNIQUE

20. TONE BUILDER

21. FLEXIBILITY STUDY

22. TECHNIQUE TRAX

△ 5th fret A string

△ 5th fret D string △

23. CHORALE

Johann Sebastian Bach

Andante

p

▽ 5th fret A string   ▽ 5th fret A string

mf   *p*

24. GRANDFATHER'S CLOCK

Henry C. Work

Allegro

mf

f   *p*

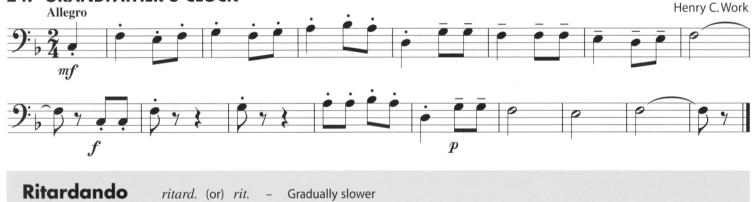

Ritardando   *ritard.* (or) *rit.* – Gradually slower

25. GLOW WORM

Paul Lincke

Allegretto ◁ *Usually a little slower than Allegro, and with a lighter style.*

1.

mf   △ 5th fret D string

2.

rit. ◁ *Watch your director.*

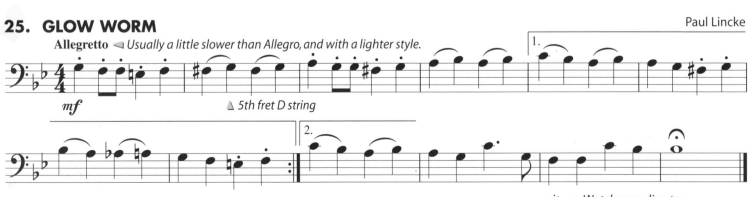

26. ALMA MATER – New Note

A.C. Weekes, W.M. Smith, H.S. Thompson

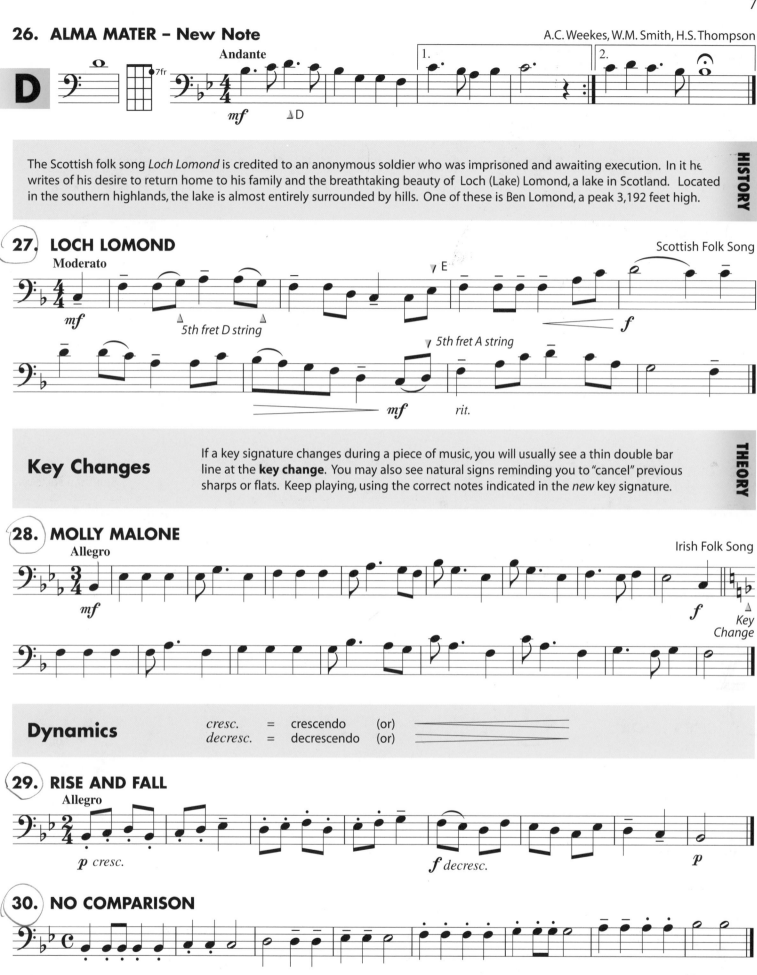

The Scottish folk song *Loch Lomond* is credited to an anonymous soldier who was imprisoned and awaiting execution. In it he writes of his desire to return home to his family and the breathtaking beauty of Loch (Lake) Lomond, a lake in Scotland. Located in the southern highlands, the lake is almost entirely surrounded by hills. One of these is Ben Lomond, a peak 3,192 feet high.

27. LOCH LOMOND

Scottish Folk Song

Key Changes

If a key signature changes during a piece of music, you will usually see a thin double bar line at the **key change**. You may also see natural signs reminding you to "cancel" previous sharps or flats. Keep playing, using the correct notes indicated in the *new* key signature.

28. MOLLY MALONE

Irish Folk Song

Dynamics

cresc. = crescendo (or)
decresc. = decrescendo (or)

29. RISE AND FALL

30. NO COMPARISON

31. SIGHTREADING CHALLENGE

Remember the S-T-A-R-S guidelines.

THEORY

¢ **Time Signature**
Cut Time (Alla Breve)

𝄢¢ or 𝄢 2/2 = **2 beats** per measure
= **Half** note gets one beat

𝅝 = 2 beats
𝅗𝅥 = 1 beat
♩ = ½ beat

32. RHYTHM RAP *Clap the rhythm while counting and tapping.*

33. A CUT ABOVE

34. TWO-FOUR YANKEE DOODLE
American Folk Song

35. CUT TIME YANKEE DOODLE
American Folk Song

36. MARIANNE
Jamaican Folk Song

37. THE VICTORS
Louis Elbel

38. ESSENTIAL CREATIVITY *Write this example in cut time ¢ before playing.*

Dynamics

mp — *mezzo piano* (moderately soft)

These are the four dynamic levels you've learned.

p — mp — mf — f

39. A - ROVING

Moderato

mp   *f*   *mp*

Syncopation

Syncopation occurs when an accent or emphasis is given to a note that is not on a strong beat. This type of "off-beat" feel is common in many popular and classical styles.

THEORY

40. RHYTHM RAP

Clap

1 & 2 & 1 & 2 & 1 & 2 & 1 & 2 & 1 & 2 & 1 & 2 & 1 & 2 & 1 & 2 &

41. IN SYNC

1 & 2 & 1 & 2 & 1 & 2 & 1 & 2 & 1 & 2 & 1 & 2 & 1 & 2 & 1 & 2 &

42. LA ROCA

Moderato   Puerto Rican Folk Song

f   *mp*   *f*   *f*

American composer **George M. Cohan** (1878–1942) was also a popular author, producer, director and performer. He helped develop a popular form of American musical theater now known as musical comedy. He is also considered to be one of the most famous composers of American patriotic songs, earning the Congressional Medal of Honor in 1917 for his song *Over There*. Many of his songs became morale boosters when the United States entered World War I in that same year.

HISTORY

43. ESSENTIAL ELEMENTS QUIZ – YOU'RE A GRAND OLD FLAG

Words and Music by George M. Cohan

March Style

mf   *mp*   *cresc.*   *f*   *mp*   *cresc.*   *f*

10

New Key Signature

This key signature indicates your **Key of C** (no sharps or flats).

44. KEY MOMENT – New Note *Try the C Scale without using open strings.*

45. THE MINSTREL BOY

Irish Folk Song

46. CLOSE CALL – New Note

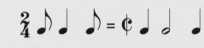

47. VICTORY MARCH

M. J. Shea

Cut Time Syncopation

Compare the notation of the melody below with *Victory March* above. Should they sound the same?

48. WINNING STREAK

M. J. Shea

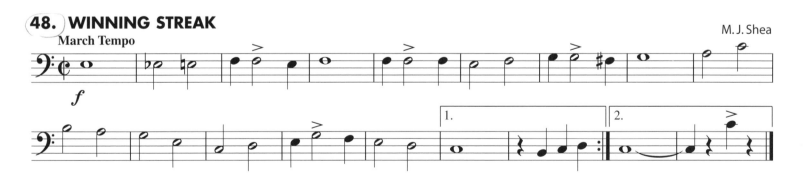

49. SIGHTREADING CHALLENGE *Remember the S-T-A-R-S guidelines.*

PERFORMANCE SPOTLIGHT

56. WARM-UP CHORALE

J. S. Bach/Arr. by John Higgins

57. THE THUNDERER – Band Arrangement

John Philip Sousa
Arr. by John Higgins

Reproduced by Permission of Boosey & Hawkes Music Publishers Ltd.

58. HILL AND GULLY RIDER – Band Arrangement

Jamaican Folk Song
Arr. by John Higgins

59. SHENANDOAH – Band Arrangement

American Folk Song
Arr. by John Higgins

PERFORMANCE SPOTLIGHT

60. LAS MAÑANITAS – Band Arrangement

Mexican Folk Song
Arr. by John Higgins

61. RONDEAU – Band Arrangement

Jean-Joseph Mouret
Arr. by John Higgins

D.S. al Fine–Go back to the sign (𝄋) and play until **Fine**. ▼

62. ROCK.COM – Encore Band Arrangement

John Higgins

Rallentando   *rall.* – Gradually slower (same as ritardando)

75. SIMPLE SONG – Duet

76. LINE DANCE

77. TECHNIQUE TRAX

78. THE GALWAY PIPER

Irish Reel

79. MANHATTAN BEACH MARCH

John Philip Sousa

Reproduced by Permission of Boosey & Hawkes Music Publishers Ltd.

80. SIGHTREADING CHALLENGE   *Remember the S-T-A-R-S guidelines.*

DAILY WARM-UPS

87. TONE BUILDER *Play at a very slow tempo.*

88. FLEXIBILITY STUDY

89. TECHNIQUE TRAX *Use A♭ major scale fingering.*

90. CHORALE

Johann Sebastian Bach

French composer **Georges Bizet** (1838–1875) entered the Paris Conservatory to study music when he was only ten years old. There he won many awards for voice, piano, organ, and composition. Bizet's best known composition is the opera *Carmen,* which was first performed in 1875. *Carmen* tells the story of a band of Gypsies, soldiers, smugglers, and outlaws. Originally criticized for its realism on stage, it was soon hailed as the most popular French opera ever written.

91. TOREADOR SONG (from CARMEN)

Georges Bizet

92. LA CUMPARSITA
Moderato
G. Rodriguez

5th fret D string

Enharmonics

quiz

93. THE YELLOW ROSE OF TEXAS
Check the key signature. Use A♭ major scale fingering.

American Folk Song

Moderato
mf

E♭ Major Scale Fingering

THEORY

94. SCALE STUDY – New Note
Try E♭ major scale fingering.

E♭ Scale

▼ E♭

▼ Check rhythm

Until 1974 Australia's official national anthem was *God Save The Queen*. A competition was held in 1973 to compose a new anthem, but none of the entries met with the judges' approval. Finally the government asked the public to vote, choosing from among Australia's 3 most popular patriotic songs. After easily defeating *Waltzing Matilda* and *God Save The Queen*, *Advance Australia Fair* was officially declared the national anthem of Australia on April 19, 1974.

HISTORY

95. ADVANCE AUSTRALIA FAIR
Peter Dodds McCormick

Maestoso
f

mp   cresc.

f

rit.   a tempo

△ Notes on D string   △ Resume previous tempo

96. ESSENTIAL CREATIVITY
Arrange the melody of "America (My Country 'Tis Of Thee)" for your instrument. Write out the first line (6 measures). Your first note is F. ADD: Key signature—key of F • Time signature—3/4 • Tempo and dynamic markings.

Play the completed line on your instrument to hear your own version.

97. AMERICAN PATROL

Moderato

F. W. Meacham

98. ARIA (from MARRIAGE OF FIGARO)

Moderato

Wolfgang Amadeus Mozart

HISTORY

American composer **John Philip Sousa** (1854–1932) was best known for his brilliant band marches. Sousa wrote 136 marches, including *The Stars and Stripes Forever,* which was declared the official march of the United States of America in 1987.

99. THE STARS AND STRIPES FOREVER

John Philip Sousa

March Tempo

Check rhythm

△ *5th fret D string*

17

△ *Use E♭ major scale fingering.*

100. SIGHTREADING CHALLENGE *Use A♭ major scale fingering. Remember the S-T-A-R-S guidelines.*

Moderato

6/8 Time Signature

$\frac{6}{8}$ = **6 beats** per measure
= **Eighth** note gets one beat

♪ = 1 beat   ♩ = 2 beats
♩. = 3 beats   ♩. = 6 beats

6/8 time is usually played with a slight emphasis on the **1st** and **4th** beats of each measure. This divides the measure into 2 groups of 3 beats each. In faster music, these two primary beats will make the music feel like it's counted "in 2."

101. RHYTHM RAP — *Clap the rhythm while counting and tapping.*

102. LAZY DAY

103. ROW YOUR BOAT

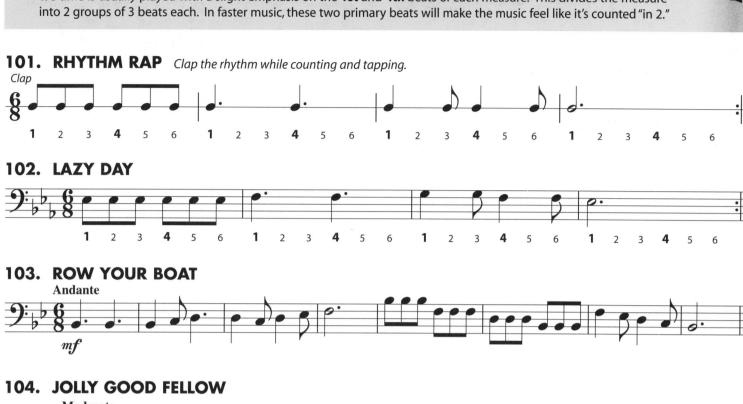

104. JOLLY GOOD FELLOW

105. CHANSON

French Folk Song

106. ESSENTIAL ELEMENTS QUIZ – WHEN JOHNNY COMES MARCHING HOME

American Folk Song

Count: **1** 2 3 **4** 5 6

THEORY

More Enharmonics

Remember that notes which sound the same but have different letter names are called **enharmonics.** These are some common enharmonics that you'll use in the exercises below.

More Chromatics

The smallest distance between two notes is a half-step, and a scale made up of consecutive half-steps is a **chromatic scale.** These are usually written with **enharmonic** notes—sharps when going up and flats when going down.

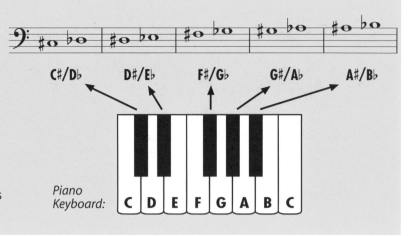

Piano Keyboard:

---

107. CHROMATIC SCALE

Practice slowly until you are sure of all the fingerings.

△ Eb Enharmonic   △ Ab Enharmonic

---

108. TECHNIQUE TRAX

HISTORY

A **Habañera** is a Cuban dance and song form in slow 2/4 meter. It is named after the city of Havana, the capital of Cuba. Made popular in the New World in the early 19th Century, it was later carried over to Spain. There the rhythms of the Habañera were incorporated into many styles of Latin music. One of the most famous Habañeras is heard in Bizet's *Carmen,* written in 1875.

---

109. HABAÑERA (from CARMEN)

Andante   Georges Bizet

---

110. CHROMATIC CRESCENDO

Moderato

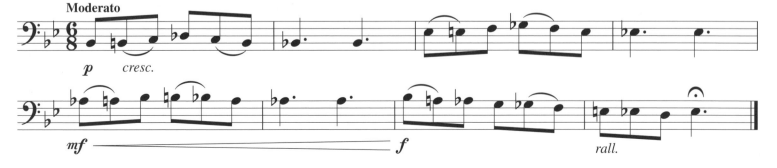

111. TURKISH MARCH (from THE RUINS OF ATHENS)

Ludwig van Beethoven

112. THE OVERLANDER

Australian Folk Song

113. STACCATO STUDY

114. YANKEE DOODLE DANDY

Words and Music by George M. Cohan

115. SIGHTREADING CHALLENGE

Remember the **S-T-A-R-S** guidelines:
S – Sharps or flats in the key signature, **T** – Time signature and tempos, **A** – Accidentals, **R** – Rhythm, **S** – Signs

24

THEORY

Triplets

A **triplet** is a group of **3** notes played in the space of **2**. In $\frac{2}{4}$, $\frac{3}{4}$, or $\frac{4}{4}$ time, an eighth note triplet is spread evenly across one beat.

= 1 beat

1 trip-let 2 trip-let

116. RHYTHM RAP

117. THREE TO GET READY

118. TRIPLET STUDY

119. MARCH (from THE NUTCRACKER) – Duet

Peter I. Tchaikovsky

120. ESSENTIAL ELEMENTS QUIZ – THEME FROM FAUST

Charles Gounod

F Major Scale Fingering

121. SCALE STUDY – New Notes *Try F major scale fingering.*

122. OVER THE RIVER AND THROUGH THE WOODS *Try F major scale fingering.* American Folk Song

123. RHYTHM RAP

124. ON THE MOVE

125. HIGHER GROUND

126. ESSENTIAL ELEMENTS QUIZ

HISTORY

The first known printing of the lyrics and music to **The Marines' Hymn** dates from August 1, 1918. An unknown author is believed to have taken the opening words of the song from the words on the Marine Corps flag, "From the halls of Montezuma to the shores of Tripoli." The music was taken from "Genevieve de Brabant," by the operetta composer Jacques Offenbach.

127. THE MARINES' HYMN

D.S. al Fine

Play until you see the **D.S. al Fine**. Then go back to the sign (𝄋) and play until the word **Fine**. **D.S.** is the abbreviation for **Dal Segno**, or "from the sign," and **Fine** means "the end."

128. D.S. MARCH *Use E♭ major scale fingering.*

Accelerando

accel. – Gradually faster.

129. CAN–CAN

Jacques Offenbach

accel.

△ *Watch your director.*

130. TARANTELLA

Italian Folk Song

f ▷ *Pick-up*   *mf*

The **waltz** is a dance in moderate 3/4 time which developed around 1800 from the Ländler, an Austrian peasant dance. Austrian composer **Johann Strauss, Jr.** (1825–1899) composed over 400 waltzes. These include such famous pieces as *The Blue Danube, Tales From the Vienna Woods* and *Emperor Waltz*.

131. EMPEROR WALTZ

Johann Strauss, Jr.

Andantino ◁ *Tempo between Andante and Moderato.*

△ *rit.*
6th fret D string

Legato Style

legato – Played in a smooth, connected style.

132. ENGLISH DANCE – Duet

Johann Christian Bach

133. ESSENTIAL ELEMENTS QUIZ – BRITISH GRENADIERS

Traditional

28

134. NASSAU BOUND

Bahamian Folk Song

Count ▶ 1 & 2 & 3 & 4 &

135. UNFINISHED SYMPHONY THEME

Franz Schubert

136. RHYTHM STUDY

Measure Repeat ⁄. Repeat the previous measure once for each **Measure Repeat** sign.

137. COUNTRY GARDENS *Use E♭ major scale fingering.*

English Folk Song

10th fret G string   Measure Repeat

rall.

138. JOSHUA

African-American Spiritual

139. LISTEN TO THE MOCKINGBIRD

Alice Hawthorne

Moderato

mf ▷ Pick-up

140. ANCHORS AWEIGH

Capt. A.H. Miles and C.A. Zimmerman

March Tempo

141. GREENSLEEVES *Use A♭ major scale fingering.*

English Folk Song

Andante

mf △ 8th fret G string

rit.

142. THE LONG CLIMB

△ Measure Repeat

143. THE BLUE BELLS OF SCOTLAND

Scottish Folk Song

Moderato

THEORY

Major and Minor

The scales you've already learned are called **Major** scales. They all follow the same pattern, with **half-steps** between notes 3–4 and between notes 7–8.

Natural Minor scales follow a different pattern, with **half-steps** between notes 2–3 and 5–6. The **G Minor** scale uses the same key signature as **B♭ Major**.

Another type of minor scale is called **Harmonic Minor**, which adds an accidental to raise the **7th** note by a half-step. Compare the scales on the right.

See page 37 for additional minor scales.

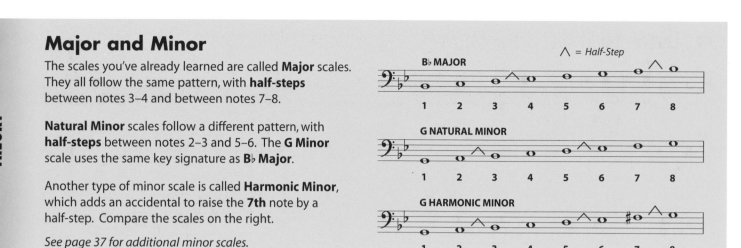

144. NATURAL MINOR SCALE

145. FINALE FROM "NEW WORLD SYMPHONY"

Antonin Dvořák

146. HARMONIC MINOR SCALE

147. HUNGARIAN DANCE NO. 5

Johannes Brahms

148. POMP AND CIRCUMSTANCE (LAND OF HOPE AND GLORY)

Edward Elgar

PERFORMANCE SPOTLIGHT

D.S. al Coda Play until you see the **D.S. al Coda**. Then go back to the sign (𝄋) and play until the **Coda Sign** ("To Coda" ⊕). Skip directly to the **Coda** and play until the end.

149. SIMPLE GIFTS – Band Arrangement

Shaker Folk Song
Arr. by John Higgins

150. SEMPER FIDELIS – Band Arrangement

John Philip Sousa
Arr. by John Higgins

PERFORMANCE SPOTLIGHT

151. DANNY BOY – Band Arrangement

Irish Folk Song
Arr. by John Higgins

152. TAKE ME OUT TO THE BALL GAME – Band Arrangement

By Jack Norworth and Harry von Tilzer
Arr. by John Higgins

PERFORMANCE SPOTLIGHT

153. SERENGETI (AFRICAN RHAPSODY) – Band Arrangement

John Higgins

RUBANK® STUDIES

154. CHORALE

155. CHORALE

156. CHORALE

157. CHORALE

158. CHORALE

KEY OF B♭

159.

160.

161.

162.

RUBANK® STUDIES

KEY OF E♭

163. *Use E♭ major scale fingering.*

164. *Use E♭ major scale fingering.*

165.

166. *Use E♭ major scale fingering.*

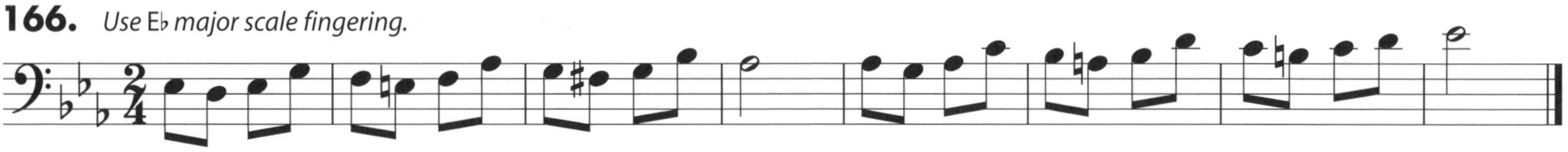

KEY OF F

167. *Use F major scale fingering.*

168.

169.

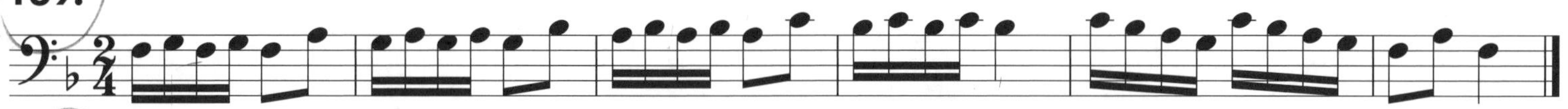

170. *Use F major scale fingering.*

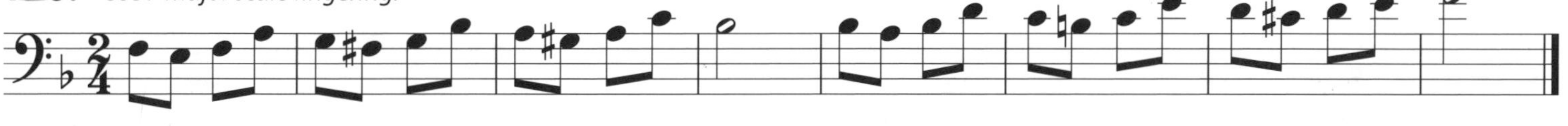

RUBANK® STUDIES

KEY OF A♭

RUBANK® STUDIES

KEY OF G MINOR

INDIVIDUAL STUDY – Electric Bass

187. LOW NOTE EXCURSION – New Note

CD Track 56

188. LOW ENHARMONIC STUDY – New Note

CD Track 57

189. MELODY PATTERNS

CD Track 58

190. ARPEGGIO CHALLENGE

CD Track 59

191. STUDY IN A♭ *Use A♭ major scale fingering.*

CD Track 60

192. CHROMATIC ETUDE

CD Track 61

INDIVIDUAL STUDY – Electric Bass

193. TECHNIQUE BUILDER #1

194. TECHNIQUE BUILDER #2

195. TECHNIQUE BUILDER #3

196. TRIPLET ETUDE

197. BASIC BLUES PATTERNS

198. BLUES PATTERNS WITH 6ths & 7ths

199. CHROMATIC BLUES PATTERNS

INDIVIDUAL STUDY – Electric Bass

Solo with Piano Accompaniment

You can perform this solo with the piano accompaniment on the following page.

200. **IN THE HALL OF THE MOUNTAIN KING from "Peer Gynt Suite" – Electric Bass Solo**

CD Track 69
Edvard Grieg
Arr. by G. E. Holmes

INDIVIDUAL STUDY – Electric Bass

200. IN THE HALL OF THE MOUNTAIN KING from "Peer Gynt Suite" – Piano accompaniment

CD Track 70

Edvard Grieg
Arr. by G. E. Holmes

RHYTHM STUDIES

RHYTHM STUDIES

CREATING MUSIC

THEORY

Theme and Variation

Theme and Variation is a technique used by composers and arrangers to create interesting musical ideas that are "varied" from an established melody, or "theme." Play the following theme and two variations to hear how the arranger has created new phrases based on the original melody.

1. THEME

"Simple Gifts"

VARIATION 1 *Adding some notes • Changing some rhythms*

VARIATION 2 *Removing notes • Changing rhythms • Adding accents • Adding notes*

2. THEME AND YOUR VARIATION *Write your own variation of this theme. Use your instrument to hear and try different ideas.*

Theme "Oh, Susanna"

Your Variation

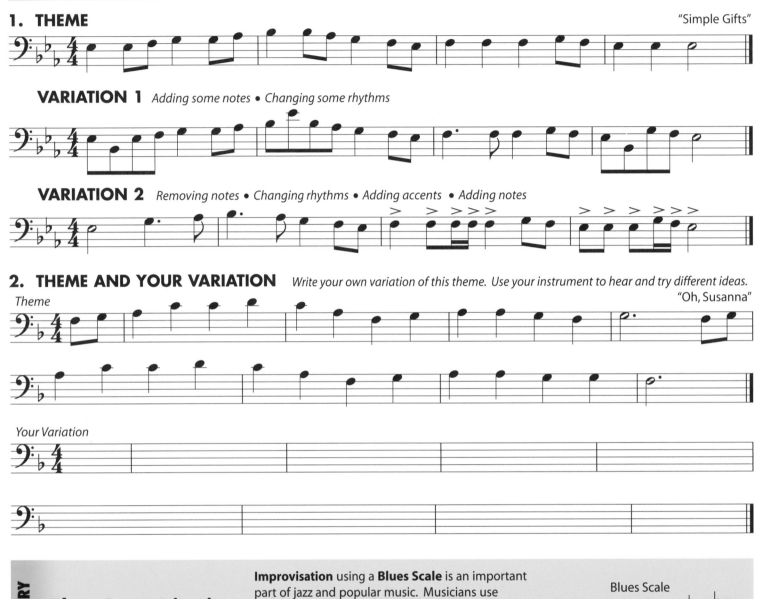

THEORY

Blues Improvisation

Improvisation using a **Blues Scale** is an important part of jazz and popular music. Musicians use combinations of these notes and various rhythms to create their own spontaneous solos over a 12 measure progression of chords.

Blues Scale

3. LET'S JAM *Use the indicated notes from the Blues Scale to create your own solo to play with the accompaniment (Line B).*

You can mark your progress through the book on this page. Fill in the stars as instructed by your band director.

ESSENTIAL
ELEMENTS
2000

STAR ACHIEVER

NAME_____

1.   Page 2–4, Review
2.   Page 5, Sightreading Challenge, No. 19
3.   Page 6, Daily Warm-Ups
4.   Page 7, Sightreading Challenge, No. 31
5.   Page 8, Essential Creativity, No. 38
6.   Page 9, EE Quiz, No. 43
7.   Page 10, Sightreading Challenge, No. 49
8.   Page 11, EE Quiz, No. 55
9.   Page 12–13, Performance Spotlight
10.   Page 15, EE Quiz, No. 74
11.   Page 16, Sightreading Challenge, No. 80
12.   Page 18, Daily Warm-Ups
13.   Page 19, Essential Creativity, No. 96
14.   Page 20, Sightreading Challenge, No. 100
15.   Page 21, EE Quiz, No. 106
16.   Page 22, Chromatic Scale, No. 107
17.   Page 23, Sightreading Challenge, No. 115
18.   Page 24, EE Quiz, No. 120
19.   Page 25, EE Quiz, No. 126
20.   Page 27, EE Quiz, No. 133
21.   Page 30, Natural Minor Scale, No. 144
22.   Page 30, Harmonic Minor Scale, No. 146
23.   Page 30, Pomp and Circumstance, No. 148
24.   Page 31, Performance Spotlight
25.   Page 32, Performance Spotlight
26.   Page 33, Performance Spotlight
27.   Page 38–39, Individual Study
28.   Page 40, Performance Spotlight

MUSIC — AN ESSENTIAL ELEMENT OF LIFE

FINGERING CHART

Instrument Care Reminders

- Be sure your amplifier is turned off before plugging-in or unplugging the audio cable connecting it to your instrument.
- When unplugging a cable, hold it by the plug (not by the wire).
- After playing, wipe off the instrument and strings with a clean soft cloth. Return the instrument to its case.
- Close all the latches on your case when the instrument is inside.
- Keep all 4 strings in tune (at normal tension) to prevent warping of the neck.
- Your case is designed to hold only specific objects. If you force anything else into the case, it may damage your instrument.

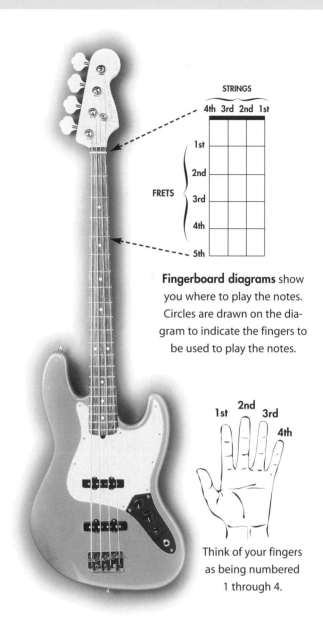

Fingerboard diagrams show you where to play the notes. Circles are drawn on the diagram to indicate the fingers to be used to play the notes.

Think of your fingers as being numbered 1 through 4.

Instrument courtesy of Yamaha Corporation of America, Band and Orchestral Division

4th string
↓

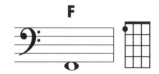

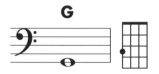

3th string

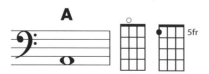

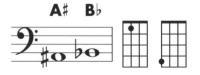

FINGERING CHART

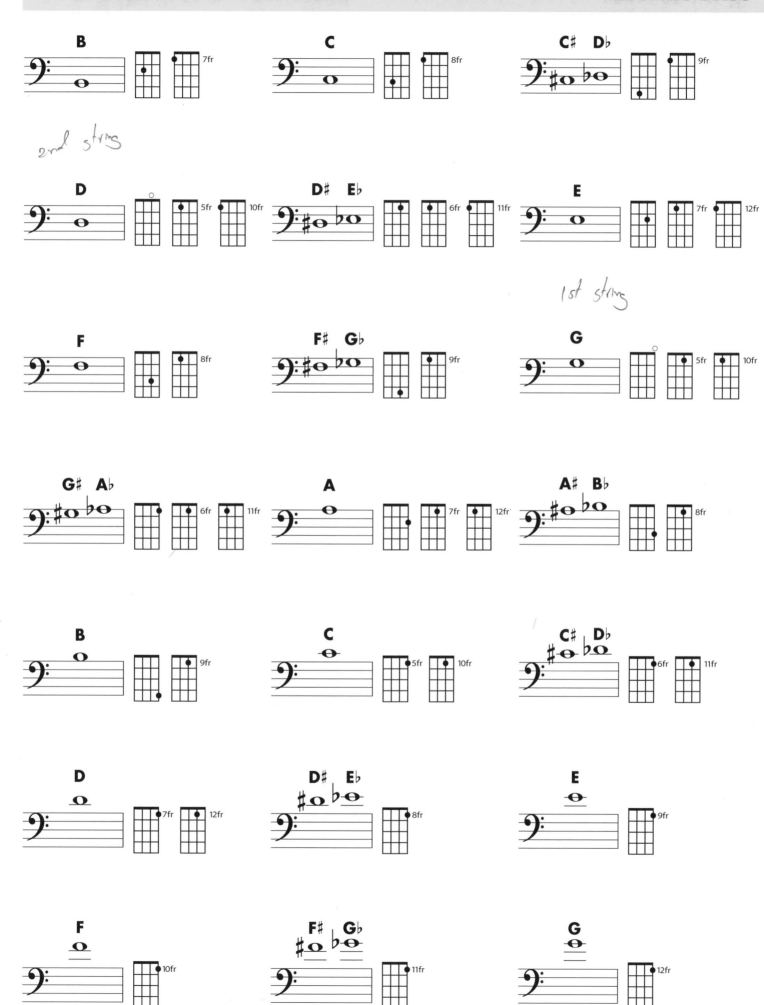

◢ REFERENCE INDEX